Katrin

RETIREMENT: A GUIDE FOR SOCIAL SECURITY

Empower Yourself To Make The Best Decisions

Thanks Scotia Wade 7-2-16

Scotia Wade

Check out other book by Scotia Wade

"100+ Budget Tips Guaranteed To Immediately Save You Money & Time"

http://www.amazon.com/dp/B01807QQNO

Disclaimer

Effort has been made to ensure that the information in this book is accurate and complete. However, the author and the publisher do not warrant the accuracy of the information, text and graphics contained within the book due to the rapidly changing nature of science, research, known and unknown facts. The author and the publisher do not hold any responsibility for errors, omissions or contrary interpretation of the subject matter herein. This book is presented solely for informational purposes only.

All information was obtained from:

Social Security website,
2015: WWW.SocialSecurity.gov

Medicare Website, 2015: www.medicare.gov

Inspirational Quotes

"You are never too old to set another goal or to dream a new dream."
-- Les Brown

"Aging is not 'lost youth' but a new stage of opportunity and strength."
-- Betty-Friedan

Dedication

This guide is dedicated to all the retiring Baby Boomers

Table of Contents

SCOTIA WADE

Introduction

I was approaching the full retirement age of 66 and I felt it was time to research exactly how Social Security worked and what needed to be done to collect full retirement payments. First I talked to people that had retired and discovered that they did not know anything about the retirement process. Researching the Social Security website was my next step. By visiting this site yearly I knew things could change. There was so much information and it was confusing. I decided to make an outline listing all the important things that was needed and also answers to questions not listed on the site. The next six months was spent obtaining information. There were so many decisions to make that I should have begun sooner. Most individuals would not do all the research needed but they would have to know the important things before filing for their Social Security. Putting all the important information into a guide would make it easier to read and more understandable.

What is the correct age to apply for social security? Can I afford to retire? Should I relocate when I retire? How do

I know I am ready? Do I have enough money? Should I continue to work? These are questions that most people ask. It actually depends on your financial stability, your health, your marital status, and how much money you will need to retire. Everyone has different needs.

This guide will provide information to enable you to answer these questions. It is impossible to answer all questions because there are so many different circumstances but you will be able to answer the most common questions. This guide will familiarize you with the important aspects of Social Security. You will be able to understand Social Security better after you read this guide; also be able to access the website SSA.gov to get answers to any other questions you may have. After you read this guide you will have enough information to make important decisions concerning your retirement.

This guide will answer the most common questions:

- When should I apply for Social Security Benefits?
- Where do I apply for Social Security Benefits?
- How do I contact the Social Security office?
- What is the best age to retire?

- When and where do I apply for Medicare?

- How will this affect my family?

These are only a few of the questions that most people have about Social Security. I am sure that there will be information in this guide that you have never considered. This guide will give all the steps necessary for applying for Social Security benefits. On Monday, November 2, 2015, President Obama signed into law the Bipartisan Budget Act of 2015. This budget act has made changes to Social Security and Medicare. This book has been updated with the information.

Who Can Apply for Retirement Benefits?

You can apply for retirement benefits or benefits as a spouse if you

- Are at least 61 years and 9 months old
- Are not currently receiving benefits on your own Social Security record
- Have not already applied for retirement benefits
- You want your benefits to start no more than 4 months in the future (Applications can't be processed if you apply for benefits more than 4 months in advance.)

Before you apply for retirement benefits, there are certain Social Security "basics" you should know about

- Your "full retirement age"

- Depending on your date of birth, that may be between age 66 and 67. This could affect the amount of your benefits and when you want the benefits to start.

- When you can start benefits

  You may start receiving benefits as early as age 62 or as late as age 70.

- Benefits are reduced for age

  Your monthly benefits will be reduced if you start them any time before "full retirement age."

- Working while you receive benefits

  If you elect to receive benefits before you reach full retirement age, you should understand how continuing to work can affect your benefits.

- Delayed retirement credits

  Delayed retirement credits may be added to your benefits if they start after your full retirement age.

- Life expectancy

  If you live to the average life expectancy for someone your age, you will receive about the same amount in lifetime benefits whether you choose to start receiving benefits at age 62, full retirement age, age 70 or any age in between.

- Age 65 remained as full retirement age until the 1983 SSA Amendments signed by President Reagan. Addressing financing needs of that time, the 1983 Amendments made numerous changes to the Social Security programs including taxation of SSA benefits and increases in the retirement age.

Age To Receive Full Social Security

Year of Birth *	Full Retirement
1937 or earlier	65
1938	65 and 2 months
1939	65 and 4 months
1940	65 and 6 months

Age To Receive Full Social Security

Year of Birth *	Full Retirement
1941	65 and 8 months
1942	65 and 10 months
1943--1954	66
1955	66 and 2 months
1956	66 and 4 months
1957	66 and 6 months
1958	66 and 8 months

Age To Receive Full Social Security

Year of Birth *	Full Retirement
1959	66 and 10 months
1960 and later	67

If you were born on January 1st of any year you should refer to the previous year. (If you were born on the 1st of the month, Social Security will figure your benefit (and your full retirement age) as if your birthday was in the previous month.)

Things to Consider Before Retirement

What is the Best Age to Retire?

If you decide to start benefits:

- Before your full retirement age, your benefit will be smaller but you will receive it for a longer period of time.

- At your full retirement age or later, you will receive a larger monthly benefit for a shorter period of time.

- The amount you receive when you first get benefits sets the base for the amount you will receive for the rest of your life.

Life Expectancy

Do you come from a long-lived family? Did your parents and grandparents all live into their 80s or 90s? If the answer is yes, and you have every reason to believe you will too, you may want to delay starting your benefits until full retirement age or later. If they didn't, you may choose to start receiving retirement benefits earlier. If you come from a long-lived family, you may need the extra money more in later years, particularly if you may outlive pensions or annuities with limits on how long they are paid.

How is your health?

If you are not in good health, you may decide to start your benefits earlier. Will you still have health insurance? If you stop working, not only will you lose your paycheck, but you may also lose valuable employer provided health insurance. **Although there are exceptions, most people will not be covered by Medicare until they reach age 65.**

Your employer should be able to tell you if you will have retiree health benefits or if you can temporarily extend your health insurance coverage after you retire. Also, if you are married and your spouse is employed, you may be able to switch to his or her health insurance.

Are you eligible for benefits on someone else's record?

If you are eligible on another record, you have additional options:

- If you qualify for benefits as a widow, widower or surviving divorced spouse on another record, you may choose to apply for survivors benefits now and delay your retirement benefit until later.

  If you delay receiving your retirement benefit until your full retirement age or later, your retirement benefit will be higher.

- If your spouse is full retirement age, he or she can apply for retirement benefits and then ask to have payments suspended. That way, you can receive a spouses benefits and he or she can continue to earn delayed retirement credits until age 70. Marries couples will not be able to do this after May 2, 2016. Couples getting this retirement benefits before May 2, 2016 will be grandfathered in.

- If you have reached your full retirement age, and are eligible for a spouses or ex-spouses benefit and your own retirement benefit, you may choose to receive only spouse's benefits. If you do that, you can delay receiving your own retirement benefit until a later date to take advantage of delayed retirement credits. You will have to provide your marriage certificate. Married couples will not be able to do this after May 2, 2016. Couples getting this retirement benefits before May 2, 2016 will be grandfathered in.

Do you have other income to support you if you decide to delay taking your benefits?

If you don't need your benefits immediately, you may decide to:

- Wait beyond full retirement age and take advantage of the delayed retirement credits.

- Choose early retirement and increase the value of your benefits by investing them instead of spending them.

Will other family members qualify for benefits with you on your record?

If your spouse or minor or disabled children will qualify for benefits with you, the value of their benefits, added to your own, may help you decide if taking your benefits sooner will be more advantageous.

When you start your retirement benefits it may also affect the amount your surviving spouse may receive. If you start your benefits:

- Before full retirement age, Social Security cannot pay your surviving spouse the full benefit amount from your record. The maximum survivors benefit is limited to what you would receive if you were still alive.

- After full retirement age, your surviving spouse may receive your full benefit amount plus any accumulated <u>delayed retirement credits</u>.

Accidents or unexpected changes in your circumstances can't be ruled out, so your final decision may be based on your "best guess" about your future. You will have to submit your marriage certificate.

Where to apply for Social Security Retirement Benefits

You can sign up for Social Security benefits on line at SSA.gov, at your local office or by phone at 1-800-772-1213. To collect your full retirement benefits, apply to Social Security three to four months before you wish to receive your first payment. Before you begin receiving your Social Security Retirement benefits, you will be sent a letter telling you when your payments start and how much you will get. Your first Social Security Retirement payment will be made for the first full month after you applied or became eligible for Social Security Retirement benefits.

The retirement toolkit http://www.dol.gov/ebsa/pdf/retirementtoolkit.pdf includes a list of publications and interactive tools to help in your planning, plus information on how to contact Social Security with your specific questions. It is important to start early and be well informed so you can make timely decisions and, if necessary, make changes while you still have time before retirement.

Determining When to Apply for Social Security Retirement Benefits

You need 40 credits (4 credits per year for 10 years) to be eligible for Social Security. If you did not work very much during your lifetime, you may have to spend time accumulating credits before you apply for retirement benefits. You can review your social security benefits on SSA.gov website.

You can begin drawing your Social Security when you reach your full retirement age but you can continue working and you will not be penalized for the amount of money you will earn.

You will still be paying social security from your salary and that can also increase your monthly payments.

Each January, your payments will increase automatically if the cost of living has gone up. Example, if the cost of living has increased by 2 percent, your benefits also will increase by 2 percent. Social Security will notify you in advance of your new amount.

Retiring at 62 is still an option but your payments will be less than if you retired at your full retirement age. If your full retirement age is 66 you may receive 65% of your full retirement benefits at age 62. If your full retirement age is 67, you may receive 70 percent of your full retirement benefits at age 62. The highest monthly amount for full retirement is $2,663.

If you are an individual who plans on working during retirement, there are a few factors you should consider.

If you have not reached full retirement age Social Security will deduct $1 for every $2 you earn above the annual limit ($15,720 in 2015). In the year you reach your full retirement age, Social Security reduces your benefits $1 for every $3 you earn over a different limit ($41,880 in 2015) until the month you reach full retirement age. Once you reach your full retirement age, you keep all of your benefits no matter how much you earn.

Sometimes people who retire in mid-year already have earned more than the yearly earnings limit. That is why a special monthly rule applies to earnings for one year, usually the first year of retirement. Under this rule, you can get full Social Security benefits for any whole month you earn under a certain limit, regardless of your yearly earnings. In 2015, Social Security consider a person younger than full retirement age (age 66 for people born in 1943-1954) retired, if monthly earnings are $1,310 or less. For example, John Smith retires at age 62 on August 30, 2015. He will make $45,000 through August. He takes a part-time job beginning in September, earning $500 a month. Although his earnings for the year substantially exceed the 2015 limit ($15,720), he will receive a Social Security payment for September through December. This is because his earnings in those months are less than $1,310, the special "first year of retirement" monthly limit for people younger than full retirement age. If Mr. Smith earns over $1,310 in any of those months (September through December), he won't receive a benefit for that month. Beginning in 2016, only the yearly limits will apply to him because he will be beyond his first year of retirement and have already used the special monthly rule during that year. If you're self-employed, Social Security bases the monthly limit on whether you perform substantial services in your business. In general, if you work over 45 hours a month in self employment, you won't get benefits for that month.

Wages count toward the earnings limit when they're earned, not when they're paid. If you have income you earned in one year, but the payment was deferred to a following year, these earnings won't count for the year you receive them. Some examples of deferred income include accumulated sick or vacation pay, bonuses, stock options, and other deferred compensation. If you receive wages in one year for work you did in previous years, you should contact Social Security. They have arrangements with the Internal Revenue Service to have employers report some types of deferred compensation on the Form W-2. These amounts are in the box labeled, "Nonqualified plans." Social Security will subtract the amount shown in the box from your total earnings to decide which earnings Social Security will count for that year.

If you're self-employed, income counts when you receive it—not when you earn it—except if it's paid in a year after you become entitled to Social Security and was earned before you became entitled to Social Security. For example, if you started getting Social Security in June 2014 and you receive some money in February 2015 for work you did before June 2014, it won't count against your 2015 earnings limit. If the money you receive in February 2015 was for work you did after June 2014, however, it will count against your 2015 earnings limit.

Because your earnings may affect your Social Security benefits, Social Security needs to know how much you earn during the year. Usually, Social Security gets that information from the earnings your employer reports on your W-2 and your self-employment earnings reported on your income tax return.

You need to report your earnings to Social Security after the end of the year only if:

—You're eligible for the special monthly rule and you earned less than the monthly limit (if so, let Social Security know so they can pay you benefits for that month)

—Some or all of the earnings shown on your W-2 were not earned in the year reported

—Your wages were over the limit, and you also had a net loss in self-employment

—Your W-2 shows employer-reported wages that you'll include on a self-employment tax return (ministers, for example)

—You filed a self-employment tax return, but you did not perform any services in your business, or you file your tax return by fiscal year

—You're a farmer, and you get federal agricultural program payments, or you have income from carryover crops

— Social Security withheld some benefits, but you had no earnings for the year, or your earnings were less than you told Social Security

If you get Supplemental Security Income (SSI) payments in addition to your Social Security benefits, you must report all of your earnings.

If Social Security has to adjust your benefit amount based on your report, they will tell you. Reviewing the information is important. About mid-year, Social Security may send you a letter asking you to estimate your current and next year's earnings. Your estimates will help Social Security avoid paying you too much or too little in benefits

If other family members get benefits on your record, your earnings may affect the total family benefits. But, if you get benefits as a family member, your earnings affect only your benefits. When you work, you should save your pay stubs. If during the year, you see your earnings will be different from what you estimated, you should call Social Security to revise the estimate. This will help

Social Security pay you the correct amount of Social Security benefits.

The Social Security administration does recalculate your benefits once you reach full retirement age, leaving out those months you did not receive benefits.

There is a Social Security calculator tool that can help when comparing different situations. http://www.ssa.gov/planners/benefitcalculators.html

Receiving Your Payment

Social Security benefits are paid monthly. The benefits are paid in the month following the month for which they are due. For example, you would receive your July benefit in August.

All Social Security payments are paid once a month by direct deposit, the Direct Express® Card Program and Electronic Transfer Account. You can sign up for direct deposit by contacting your bank or Social Security. Direct Express Card Program deposits are made directly to the card account. You can call Treasury Electronic Payment Solution Contact Center at 1-800-333-1795 or sign up online at www.Godirect.org. An Electronic Transfer Account is a low-cost federally insured account that lets you enjoy the security and convenience of automatic payments. You can contact Social Security or visit the website at www.eta-find.gov to get information about this program or to find a bank, savings and loan, or credit union near you offering this account.

If you don't receive your electronic payment on its due date, call Social Security immediately at the toll-free number, 1-800-772-1213.

If you receive an electronic payment that you know is not due you, have your financial institution return it to the U.S. Treasury Department. If you knowingly accept payments that aren't due you, you may face criminal charges.

Your Social Security checks are deposited on the second, third, or fourth Wednesday of each month, depending on your day of birth, according to the schedule below. If you receive benefits based on your spouse's work, your benefit payment date will be on your spouse's birth date.

If you receive both Social Security and SSI benefits, your Social Security payment will arrive on the third of the month and your SSI payment will arrive on the first of the month.

If you were born on the:

- 1 – 10th of the month, expect your Social Security check to be deposited on the 2nd Wednesday of each month

- 11 – 20th of the month, expect your Social Security check to be deposited on the 3rd Wednesday of each month

- 21 – 31th of the month, expect your Social Security check to be deposited on the 4th Wednesday of each month

Paying Taxes on Your Benefits

About 40 percent of all people receiving Social Security benefits have to pay taxes on their benefits. You'll have to pay taxes on your benefits if you file a federal tax return as an "individual," and your total income is more than $25,000. If you file a joint return, you'll have to pay taxes if you and your spouse have a total income that is more than $34,000. If married and filing separate returns, you probably will pay taxes on your benefits.

If parts of your benefits are taxable, how much is taxable depends on the total amount of your benefits and other income. Generally, the higher that total amount, the greater the taxable part of your benefits. Generally, up to 50% of your benefits will be taxable. However, up to 85% of your benefits can be taxable if either of the following situations applies to you.

- The total of one-half of your benefits and all your other income is more than $34,000 ($44,000 if you are married filing jointly).

- You are married filing separately and lived with your spouse at any time during the year.

To have federal taxes withheld, you can get the Form W-4V from the Internal Revenue Service by calling the toll-free telephone number, 1-800-829-3676, or by visiting their <u>website</u>. After completing and signing the form, return it to your local Social Security office by mail or in person. For more information, call the Internal Revenue Service's toll-free number, 1-800-829-3676, to ask for Publication 554, Tax Guide for seniors, and Publication 915, Social Security and Equivalent Railroad Retirement Benefits.

What You Need to Report to Social Security

Let Social Security know as soon as possible when a change listed occurs.

Failure to report a change may result in an overpayment. If you're overpaid, Social Security will recover any payments not due you. Also, if you fail to report changes in a timely way or you intentionally make a false statement, Social Security may stop your benefits. For the first violation, your benefits will stop for six months; for the second violation, 12 months; and for the third, 24 months.

You can call, write, or visit Social Security to make a report. Have your claim number handy. If you receive benefits based on your work, your claim number is the same as your Social Security number. If you receive benefits on someone else's work record, your claim number will be on any letter Social Security sends you about your benefits. Another government agency may give Social Security information you report to them, but you must also report the change to Social Security.

If your estimated earnings change

If you're working, Social Security usually asks you to estimate your earnings for the year. If later you realize your earnings will be higher or lower than you estimated, let Social Security know as soon as possible so they can adjust your benefits.

If you move

When you plan to move, tell Social Security your new address and phone number as soon as you know them. Even if you receive your benefits by direct deposit, Social Security must have your correct address so they can send letters and other important information to you. Social Security will stop your benefits if they can't contact you. You can change your address at SSA.gov by opening a "My Social Security Account."Or you can call

1-800-772-1213 and use the automated system. If any family members who are getting benefits are moving with you, please tell Social Security their names. Be sure you also file a change of address with your post office.

If you change direct deposit accounts

If you change financial institutions, or open a new account, you can change your direct deposit online if you have a "My Social Security Account."Or, Social Security can change your direct deposit information over the telephone, 1-800-772-1213, after they confirm your identity. Have your new and old bank account numbers handy when you call Social Security. These numbers are printed on your personal checks or account statements. This information takes about 30-60 days to change. Don't close your old account until after you make sure your Social Security benefits are being deposited into the new account.

If a person isn't able to manage funds

Sometimes a person can't manage their own money. If this happens, someone should let Social Security know. Social Security can arrange to send benefits to a relative, other person, or organization that agrees to use the money for the well being of the person getting benefits. Social Security will call this person or organization a "representative payee." For more information, read A Guide for Representative Payees (Publication No. 05-10076). People who have "legal guardianship" or "power of attorney" for someone don't automatically qualify to be a representative payee.

If you get a pension from non-covered work

If you start receiving a pension from a job for which you did not pay Social Security taxes—for example, from the federal Civil Service Retirement System or some state or local pension systems—your Social Security benefits may need to be recalculated, and they may be reduced. You will have to tell Social Security if the amount of your pension changes.

If you get married or divorced

If you get married or divorced, your Social Security benefits may be affected, depending on the kind of benefits you receive. If Social Security stops your benefits because of marriage or remarriage, they may start them again if the marriage ends.

- If you get your own retirement benefits your benefits will continue.

- Spouse's benefits will continue if they get divorced and they are age 62 or older unless they were married less than 10 years.

- Widow's or widower's benefits will continue if they remarry when they're age 60 or older. Any other kind of benefits will stop when they get married. Your benefits may be started again if the marriage ends.

If you change your name

If you change your name—by marriage, divorce, or court order—you need to tell Social Security right away. If you don't give Social Security this information, your benefits will come under your old name and, if you have direct deposit; payments may not reach your account.

If you get benefits because you're caring for a child

If you receive benefits because you're caring for a child who is younger than age 16 or disabled, you should notify Social Security right away if the child is no longer in your care or changes address. Give Social Security the name and address of the person with whom the child is living. A temporary separation may not affect your benefits if you continue to exercise parental control over the child, but your benefits will stop if you no longer have responsibility for the child. If the child returns to your care, Social Security can start sending benefits to you again. Your benefits will end when the youngest unmarried child in your care reaches age 16, unless the child is disabled.

If someone adopts a child who is receiving benefits

When a child who is receiving benefits is adopted, let Social Security know the child's new name, the date of the adoption decree, and the adopting parent's name and address. The adoption won't cause benefits to end.

If you become a parent after you begin to receive benefits

If you become the parent of a child (including an adopted child) after you begin receiving benefits, let Social Security know so Social Security can decide whether the child is eligible for benefits.

If you have an outstanding warrant for your arrest

You must tell Social Security if you have an outstanding arrest warrant for any of the following felony offenses:

- Flight to avoid prosecution or confinement

- Escape from custody

- Flight-escape

44

You can't receive regular retirement, survivors, disability benefits, or any other payments you may be due, for any month in which there is an outstanding arrest warrant for any of these felony offenses.

If you're convicted of a criminal offense

If you get Social Security benefits and are convicted of a crime, Social Security should be notified immediately. Benefits generally aren't paid for the months a person is confined, but any family members who are eligible may continue to receive benefits.

If you've committed a crime and are confined to an institution

Benefits usually aren't paid to persons who commit a crime and are confined to an institution by court order and at public expense for more than 30 continuous days. This applies if the person has been found:

• Guilty, but insane

• Not guilty by reason of insanity or similar factors (such as mental disease, mental defect or mental incompetence)

• Incompetent to stand trial

• Sexually dangerous

If you violate a condition of parole or probation

You must tell Social Security if you're violating a condition of your probation or parole imposed under federal or state law. You can't receive Social Security benefits for any month in which you violate a condition of your probation or parole.

If you leave the United States

If you're a U.S. citizen, you can travel to or live in most foreign countries without affecting your Social Security benefits. There are, however, a few countries where Social Security can't send Social Security payments. These countries are Azerbaijan, Belarus, Cuba, Georgia,

Kazakhstan, Kyrgyzstan, Moldova, North Korea, Tajikistan, Turkmenistan, Ukraine, Uzbekistan and Vietnam. However, Social Security can make exceptions for certain eligible beneficiaries in countries other than Cuba and North Korea. For more information about these exceptions, please contact your local Social Security office. Let them know if you plan to go outside the United States for a trip that lasts 30 days or more. Tell them the name of the country or countries you plan to visit and the date you expect to leave the United States. Social Security will send you special reporting instructions and tell you how to arrange for your benefits while you're away. Be sure to let Social Security know when you return to the United States. If you aren't a U.S. citizen, and you return to live in the United States, you must provide evidence of your noncitizen status to continue receiving benefits. If you work outside the United States, different rules apply in deciding whether you can get your benefits.

If your citizenship status change

If you aren't a citizen, let Social Security know if you become a U.S. citizen or your noncitizen status changes. If your immigration status expires, you must give Social Security new evidence that shows you can continue to be in the United States lawfully.

If a beneficiary dies

Let Social Security know if a person receiving Social Security benefits dies. Social Security can't pay benefits for the month of death. That means if the person died in July, the check received in August (which is payment for July) must be returned. If the payment is by direct deposit, notify the financial institution as soon as possible so it can return any payments received after death. Family members may be eligible for Social Security survivor's benefits when a person getting benefits dies.

If you're receiving Social Security and Railroad Retirement benefits

If you're receiving both Social Security and Railroad Retirement benefits based on your spouse's work, and your spouse dies, you must tell Social Security immediately. You'll no longer be eligible to receive both benefits. You'll be notified which survivor benefit you'll receive.

Medicare

Medicare is a health insurance plan for people who are age 65 or older. When you reach full retirement age it is mandatory to apply for Medicare. If you are still working with insurance coverage or your spouse has insurance you will not have to apply. Your Medicare payments will be deducted from your retirement check. You should apply for Medicare within three months of your 65th birthday. If you are not at full retirement age you will have to make Medicare payments every 3 months. Once you no longer have other health insurance you have to apply for Medicare. You have eight months after the last day of your health care insurance. You will be penalized by permanent higher monthly Medicare payments. People who are disabled, or have permanent kidney failure or amyotrophic lateral sclerosis (Lou Gehrig's disease), can get Medicare at any age.

Medicare has four parts

Hospital insurance (Part A) helps pay for inpatient hospital care and certain follow-up services.

Medical insurance (Part B) helps pay for doctors' services, outpatient hospital care, and other medical services.

Medicare Advantage plans (Part C) are available in many areas. People with Medicare Parts A and B can choose to receive all of their health care services through a provider organization under Part C.

Prescription drug coverage (Part D) helps pay for medications doctors prescribe.

Part A: Who is eligible for hospital insurance?

Most people get hospital insurance when they turn 65. You qualify for it automatically if you're eligible for Social Security or Railroad Retirement benefits. Or you may qualify based on a spouse's (including divorced spouses) work. Others qualify because they're government employees not covered by Social Security who paid the Medicare tax. You are eligible for Medicare part A (hospital insurance) when you are 65 and usually there is no charge for that. It helps pay for inpatient hospital care and certain follow-up services. If you do not have enough work history (you have not paid enough quarters of Medicare taxes), you will have to pay a monthly premium for Part A

For Part A, each month (in 2015) you will pay:

- Nothing if you or your spouse worked and paid Medicare taxes for 10 years or more in the U.S.
- $224 if you or your spouse worked and paid Medicare taxes between 7.5 and 10 years in the U.S.
- $407 if you or your spouse worked and paid Medicare taxes for fewer than 7.5 years in the U.S.

If you get Social Security disability benefits for 24 months, you'll qualify for hospital insurance. If you get disability benefits because you have amyotrophic lateral sclerosis (Lou Gehrig's disease), you don't have to wait 24 months to qualify. Also, people who have permanent kidney failure that requires maintenance dialysis or a kidney replacement qualify for hospital insurance, if they've worked long enough or if they're the spouse or child of a person who's worked long enough.

Part B: Who can get medical insurance?

Anyone eligible for hospital insurance can get medical insurance. Part B is an optional program that isn't free. With the signing of the Bipartisan Budget Act of 2015 there will be changes in Medicare Part B premiums. Most Social Security recipients will continue to pay the same $104.90 Medicare Part B premium in 2016. People who newly enroll in Medicare Part B in 2016 will pay a slightly higher Medicare Part B premium of $121.80 per month. High income beneficiaries will pay higher Medicare Part B premiums. The Medicare Part B deductible will increase from $147 in 2015 to $166 in 2016.

Single Filer Income	Joint Filer Income	2016 Monthly Premium
Up to $85,000	Up to $170,000	$121.80 or $104.90*
$85,001 - $107,000	$170,001 - $214,000	$170.50
$107,001 - $160,000	$214,001 - $320,000	$243.60
$160,001 - $214,000	$320,001 - $428,000	$316.70
More than $214,000	More than $428,000	$389.80

* If protected by the hold-harmless provision

There is a special rule for Social Security recipients, called the "hold harmless rule," that ensures that Social Security checks will not decline from one year to the next because of increases in Medicare Part B premiums. The hold harmless rule applies to most, but not all, Social Security recipients. Most people who receive Social Security disability or retirement benefits and Medicare Part B (coverage for doctor visits) are eligible for protection under this rule. Whether this rule comes into play in a particular year depends on the amount of COLA and the Medicare Part B premium increase.

Part C: Who can get Medicare Advantage plans?

Anyone who has Medicare hospital insurance (Part A) and medical insurance (Part B) can join a Medicare Advantage plan. Medicare Advantage plans include:

- Medicare managed care plans

- Medicare Preferred Provider organization (PPO) plans

- Medicare private fee-for-service plans

- Medicare specialty plans

As well as your Part B premium, you might have to pay another monthly premium because of the extra benefits the Medicare Advantage plan offers. If you decide to join a Medicare Advantage plan, you use the health card that you get from your Medicare Advantage plan provider for your health care. You can enroll in a Medicare Advantage plan during your initial enrollment period the first time you're eligible for Medicare. You can also enroll during the annual Medicare open enrollment period from October 15 – December 7 each year. The effective date for the enrollment is January 1 of the upcoming year. There are also special enrollment periods for some situations.

Part D: Who can get Medicare prescription drug coverage?

Anyone who has Medicare hospital insurance (Part A), medical insurance (Part B), or a Medicare Advantage plan (Part C) is eligible for prescription drug coverage (Part D). Prescription insurance is optional, and you pay an extra monthly premium for the coverage. Some people with higher incomes pay higher premiums.

"Extra Help" with Medicare prescription costs

If you have limited income and resources, you may qualify for "Extra Help" to pay for the annual deductibles, monthly premiums, and prescription co-payments related to the Medicare prescription drug program (Part D).Social Security's role is to help you understand how you may qualify and to process your application for "Extra Help".

You automatically qualify and don't need to apply for "Extra Help" if you have Medicare and meet one of the following conditions:

- Have full Medicaid coverage
- Have Supplemental Security Income (SSI)
- Take part in a state program that pays your Medicare premiums

These income and resource limits usually change each year. For more information about getting help with your prescription drug costs, call Social Security's toll-free number 1-800-772-1213 or visit SSA.gov. You can also apply online at http://www.socialsecurity.gov/extrahelp.

Help with Medicare expenses for people with low income

If you have a low income and few resources, your state may pay your Medicare premiums and, in some cases, other "out-of-pocket" medical expenses, such as deductibles and coinsurance. To qualify, you must have

Medicare hospital insurance (Part A) and have limited income and resources. Only your state can decide whether you qualify for help under this program. For more information, contact your state or local medical assistance (Medicaid) agency, social services, or welfare office. Visit www.medicare.gov/contacts or call 1-800-MEDICARE (TTY 1-877-486-2048) to get their phone number.

Spouse and Family Benefits

Whether a spouse has never worked under social security, your spouse may be able to get benefits if one of the spouses is at least 62 years of age and you are receiving or eligible for retirement or disability benefits. He or she can also qualify for Medicare at age 65. You will have to submit your marriage certificate.

If a spouse is under full retirement age and qualified on his or her own record, Social Security will pay that amount first. But if he or she also qualified for a higher amount as a spouse, they'll get a combination of benefits that equals the higher amount. If she or he begins receiving benefits:

- Between age 62 and their full retirement age, the amount will be permanently reduced by a percentage based on the number of months up to his or her full retirement age

- If your spouse is under full retirement age and

- o works while receiving benefits, his or her benefits may be affected by the <u>retirement earnings test</u>

- o also qualifies on his or her own record, his or her application will include both benefits

- At his or her full retirement age, their benefit as a spouse can be equal to one-half of your full retirement amount. The benefits for your spouse do not include any delayed retirement credit you many receive

- If you and your spouse are full retirement age and your spouse will receive a pension for work not covered by Social Security such as government of foreign employment, the amount of his or her Social Security benefits on your record may be reduced

- Your husband or wife can also receive just the spouse's benefit at any age if he or she is caring for your child who is also receiving benefits

- Your spouse would receive these benefits until your child reaches age 16, at that time, the child's benefits continues, but your spouse's benefits stop unless he or she is old enough to receive benefits base on their age

- Benefits paid to your spouse will not decrease your retirement benefit. In fact, the value of the benefits he or she may receive, added to your own, may help you decide if taking your benefits sooner many be more advantageous

If you are full retirement age, you can apply for retirement benefits and then request the payments suspended. That way, your spouse can receive a spouse's benefit and you continue to earn delayed retirement credits until age 70.

Only one member of a couple can apply for retirement benefits and have payments suspended so his or her current spouse can collect benefits.

If your spouse has reached full retirement age and is eligible for a spouse's benefit and his or her own retirement benefit, he or she has a choice. Your spouse can choose to receive only the spouse's benefit (1/2) when he or she applies online and delay receiving retirement benefits until a later date. If retirement benefits are delayed, a higher benefit may be received at a later date based on the effect of delayed retirement credits. This benefit will end May 2, 2016.

If you and your spouse apply online for retirement benefits at the same time, or if your spouse applies online after you start receiving benefits, Social Security will check his or her eligibility for benefits as a spouse. If he or she is qualified, the online application will automatically include a request for spousal benefits on your record.

If one of your children qualifies for benefits, there is a limit to the amount Social Security can pay your family.

The total depends on your benefit amount and the number of family members who also qualify on your record. The total varies, but generally the total amount you and your family can receive is about 150 to 180 percent of your full retirement benefit. If you have a divorced spouse who also qualified for benefits, he or she will not affect the amount of benefits you or your family may receive.

If you are divorced, your ex-spouse can receive benefits based on your record (even if you have remarried) if:

- Your marriage lasted 10 years or longer

- Your ex-spouse is unmarried

- Your ex-spouse is age 62 or older

- The benefit that your ex-spouse is entitled to receive based on his or her own work is less than the benefit he or she would receive based on your work

- You are entitled to Social Security retirement or disability benefits

- If you have not applied for retirement benefits, but can qualify for them, your ex-spouse can receive benefits on your record if you have been divorced for at least two years. You will have to provide certified copies of your divorce papers and marriage license. You should apply for copies months before you apply for Social Security if this information is in another state other than the one you are applying for Social Security. Social Security will make copies for their file and return the certified copies to you. This benefit will end May 2, 2016. Divorce persons getting this retirement benefits before May 2, 2016 will be grandfathered in.

If your divorced spouse remarries, he or she generally cannot collect benefits on your record unless their later marriage ends (whether by death, divorce or annulment).

If your divorced spouse is eligible for retirement benefits on his or her own record Social Security will pay that amount first. But if

- The benefit on your record is a higher amount; he or she will get a combination of benefits that equals that higher amount (reduced for age)

- Your divorced spouse has reached full retirement age and is eligible for a spouse's benefit and his or her own retirement benefit, he or she has a choice

Your divorced spouse can choose to receive only the divorced spouse's benefits (1/2) when he or she applies online and delay receiving retirement benefits until a later date. If retirement benefits are delayed, a higher benefit may be received at a later date based on the effect of delayed retirement credits.

If your former spouse

- Continues to work while receiving benefits, the same earnings limits apply to him or her as apply to you. If he or she is eligible for benefits this year and is also working, you can use the earnings test calculator to see how those earnings would affect those benefit payments.

- Will also receive a pension based on work not covered by Social Security, such as government or foreign work, his or her Social Security benefit on your record may be affected.

If you have a divorced spouse who also qualifies for benefits, he or she will not affect the amount of benefits you or your family may receive.

Retirement benefits for widows or widowers

You can switch to retirement benefits based on your own work if they're higher than those you receive for your deceased spouse's work. These benefits may be higher as early as age 62 or possibly as late as age 70. The rules are complex and vary depending on your situation. You need to speak to a Social Security representative about retirement benefits (or your circumstances have changed), contact your local Social Security office to discuss the choices available to you.

Benefits for children

If a child is getting benefits based on your work, there are important things you should know about his or her benefits:

When a child reaches age 18

—A child's benefits stop with the month before the child reaches age 18, unless the child is disabled or is a full-time elementary or secondary school student.

—About five months before the child's 18th birthday, the person receiving the child's benefits will get a form explaining how benefits can continue.

—A child whose benefits stopped at age 18 can have them started again, if he or she becomes disabled before reaching age 22. Benefits can also start again if the child becomes a full-time elementary or secondary school student before reaching age 19.

If a child is disabled

—A child can continue to receive benefits after age 18, if he or she has a disability. The child also may qualify for Supplemental Security Income (SSI) disability payments. Call Social Security for more information.

If a child age 18 is a student

—A child can receive benefits until age 19, if he or she continues to be a full-time elementary or secondary school student. When your child's 19th birthday occurs during a school term, their benefits can continue until completion of the term, or for two months following the 19th birthday, whichever comes first.

—Tell Social Security immediately if the student drops out of school, changes status from full-time to part-time, is expelled or suspended, or changes schools. Also tell Social Security if the student's employer pays him or her for attending school.

—Social Security sends each student a form at the start and end of the school year. Filling out the form, and returning it to Social Security, is important. Social Security can stop benefits if they don't receive the form.

—A student can keep receiving benefits during a vacation period of four months or less, if he or she plans to go back to school full time at the end of the vacation.

—A student who stops attending school can restart

benefits, if he or she returns to school full time before age 19. The student needs to contact Social Security and reapply for benefits.

How divorce affects a stepchild's benefits

If a stepchild is receiving benefits based on your work, and you and the child's parent divorce, the stepchild's benefit will end the month after the divorce becomes final. You must tell Social Security as soon as the divorce becomes final.

Supplemental Nutrition Assistance Program (Food Stamps)

You might be able to get help through the Supplemental Nutrition Assistance Program (SNAP), formerly known as food stamps. Visit http://www.fns.usda.gov/snap to find out how to apply.

Can you get Supplemental Security Income (SSI)?

If you have limited income and resources, SSI may be able to help. SSI is a federal program that Social Security manages. General revenues, not Social Security taxes, finance the SSI program. SSI pays monthly checks to people who are ages 65 or older, or who are blind or disabled. If you get SSI, you may also qualify for Medicaid, <u>Supplemental Nutrition Assistance Program</u> (SNAP), and other social services. Social Security doesn't count some income and some resources when they decide whether you're eligible for SSI. Your house and your car, for example, usually don't count as resources. Call Social Security toll free 1-800-772-1213 for more information or to apply for SSI.

Your Personal Money Accounts

If you retire and have a 401K you can withdraw your money or you can roll it over to an IRA account without paying any taxes. If you withdraw your money you will have to pay taxes that could be as much as 50% of your total amount. You can always leave your money with your company until you decide your options.

Your pension can be rolled over to an IRA account also. If you decide to withdraw your money the taxes will be very high up to 30%.

Taxable Accounts: Profits from the sale of investments, such as stocks, bonds, mutual funds and real estate, are taxed at capital-gains rates, which vary depending on how long you've owned the investments. Long-term capital-gains rates, which apply to assets you have held longer than a year, can be quite favorable: If you're in the 10% or 15% tax bracket, you'll pay 0% on those gains. Most other taxpayers pay 15% on long-term gains. Short-term capital gains are taxed at your ordinary income tax rate.

Interest on savings accounts and CDs and dividends paid by your money market mutual funds is taxed at your ordinary income rate. Interest from municipal bonds is tax-free at the federal level.

Roth IRAS that has been open for at least five years and you're 59 ½ years or older all withdrawals are tax-free. In addition, you don't have to take required minimum distributions from your Roth when you turn 70 1/2.

A portion of your Social Security benefits could be taxable. Whether or not you're taxed depends on what's known as your provisional income: your adjusted gross income plus any tax-free interest plus 50% of your benefits. If provisional income is between $25,000 and $34,000 if you're single or between $32,000 and $44,000 if you're married, up to 50% of your benefits are taxable. If it exceeds $34,000 if you're single or $44,000 if you're married, up to 85% of your benefits are taxable.

Pensions: Payments from private and government pensions are usually taxable at your ordinary income rate, assuming you made no after-tax contributions to the plan.

Annuities: If you purchased an annuity that provides income in retirement, the portion of the payment that represents your principal is tax-free; the rest is taxable. The insurance company that sold you the annuity is required to tell you what is taxable. Different rules apply if you bought the annuity with pretax funds (such as from a traditional IRA). In that case, 100% of your payment will be taxed as ordinary income.

The myRA is a new type of Roth retirement account launched in late 2015 that has no fees and is guaranteed by the government never to lose value. There is only one investment option, a Treasury savings bond with a variable interest rate that has averaged 3.19 percent over the past 10 years. The savings bond interest is not taxed while in the account and won't be taxed at all if you leave it in the account until after age 59 1/2. Savers who earn less than $131,000 for individuals and $193,000 for couples are eligible to contribute up to $5,500 per year, or $6,500 if they are age 50 or older. However, once the account balance grows to $15,000, or the account turns 30 years old, the money will be transferred to a private sector Roth IRA.

Your Right to Question the Decision Made on Your Claim

Social Security wants to be sure that you receive the Social Security benefits you qualify for. They carefully look at all of the facts before making a decision about your eligibility for benefits and the amount you can receive. If you disagree with their decision, you can appeal it. That means you can ask Social Security to look at your case again. When you ask for an appeal, Social Security will look at the entire decision, not just the part you disagree with. If Social Security decision was wrong, they will change it. There are four levels of appeal. If you're not satisfied with the decision at one level, you may appeal to the next.

The levels are:

- Reconsideration
- Hearing
- Appeals Council review
- Federal court

When to appeal

In order to file an appeal, it is important to understand the time frame during which you can ask for one. You have 60 days from the date you receive the letter telling you about Social Security decision to request an appeal. Social Security assumes you'll get their letter within five days after the date on the letter, unless you can show them you got it later. If you do not appeal within the 60-day time limit, you may lose your right to appeal and the last decision Social Security made becomes final. For example, if you do not ask for reconsideration within 60 days, you may lose your right to have your case reviewed. If you have a good reason for not appealing your case within the time limits, Social Security may give you more time. A request for more time must be made to Social Security in writing, stating the reason for the delay. If the last day to appeal falls on a Saturday, Sunday or national holiday, the time limit extends to the next workday.

How to appeal

You must request your appeal in writing. You can call Social Security and ask for the appeal form or send them a signed note with your Social Security number stating that you wish to appeal the decision in your case. If you applied for Social Security disability benefits and your application was denied, the fastest and easiest way to file an appeal of your decision is by visiting this web site. You can upload documents online to support your appeal, which will help decrease the time it takes to receive a decision from Social Security. If you live outside of the United States, now you can also appeal your Social Security disability decision online.

Your right to representation

You may choose to have someone help you with your appeal or to represent you. Your representative may be a lawyer or other qualified person familiar with you and the Social Security program. Social Security will work with your representative just as they would work with you. He or she can act for you in most Social Security matters and will receive a copy of any decisions Social

Security makes about your claim. Your representative cannot charge or collect a fee from you without first getting written approval from Social Security. If you want more information about having a representative, ask for Your Right To Representation (Publication No. 05-10075), which also is available online at the Social Security website, http://www.socialsecurity.gov.

Reconsideration

Reconsideration is a complete review of your claim by someone at Social Security (or at the state Disability Determination Services if you're appealing a disability decision); who had no part in the first decision. That person will look at all the evidence used to make the original decision, plus any new evidence. When Social Security makes a decision on your reconsideration, they will send you a letter explaining the decision.

Hearing

If you disagree with the reconsideration decision, you may ask for a hearing. The hearing will be conducted by an administrative law judge who had no part in the original decision or the reconsideration of your case. The hearing is usually held within 75 miles of your home. The administrative law judge will notify you of the time and place of the hearing. Before the hearing, Social Security may ask you to give them more evidence and to clarify information about your claim. You may look at the information in your file and give new information. At the hearing, the administrative law judge will question you and any witnesses you bring. Other witnesses, such as medical or vocational experts, may also give Social Security information at the hearing. You or your representative may question the witnesses. In certain situations, Social Security may hold your hearing by a video conference rather than in person. Social Security will let you know ahead of time if they will do this in your case. With video hearings, Social Security can make the hearing more convenient for you. Often an appearance by video hearing can be scheduled faster than an in-person one. Also, a video hearing location may be closer to your home. That might make it easier for you to have witnesses or other people accompany you. It is usually to your advantage to attend the hearing (in person or video conference). You and your representative, if you have one, should come to the hearing and explain your case. If you are unable to attend a hearing or do not wish to do so, you must tell Social Security why in writing as soon as you can. Unless the administrative law judge believes your presence is necessary to decide your case and requires you to attend, you won't have to go. Or Social Security may be able to make other arrangements for you, such as changing the time or place of your hearing. You must have a good reason for Social Security to make other arrangements. After the hearing, the judge will make a decision based on all the information in your case, including any new information you give. Social Security will send you a letter and a copy of the judge's decision.

Council Review

If you disagree with the hearing decision made by the administrative law judge, you may ask for a review by Social Security's Appeals Council. The Appeals Council looks at all requests for review, but it may deny a request if it believes the hearing decision was correct. If the Appeals Council decides to review your case, the Council will either decide your case itself or issue an order returning your case to an administrative law judge for further action. If the Appeals Council denies your request for review, Social Security will send you a letter explaining the denial. If the Appeals Council decides your case itself, Social Security will send you a copy of the decision. If the Appeals Council returns your case to an administrative law judge, Social Security will send you a letter and a copy of the order.

Federal Court

If you disagree with the Appeals Council's decision or if the Appeals Council decides not to review your case, you may file a lawsuit in a federal district court. The letter Social Security will send you about the Appeals Council's decision also will tell you how to ask a court to look at your case.

Contact Information for Social Security

Visit http://www.socialsecurity.gov anytime to apply for
benefits, open a My Social Security account, find
publications, and get answers to frequently asked
questions. Or, call Social Security toll-free at 1-800-772-
1213 (for the deaf or hard of hearing, call Social Security
TTY number, 1-800-325-0778). Social Security can
answer case specific questions from 7 a.m. to 7 p.m.,
Monday through Friday. Generally, you'll have a shorter
wait time if you call after Tuesday. Social Security treats
all calls confidentially. Social Security also wants to
make sure you receive accurate and courteous service, so
a second Social Security representative monitors some
telephone calls. Social Security can provide general
information by automated phone service 24 hours a day.
And, remember, Social Security
website, www.socialsecurity.gov, is available to you
anytime.

Contact Social Security about your payment:

Email: payment.inquiries@ssa.gov

Fax: (410) 965-9248

Postal mail:

Social Security Administration

Division of Administrative Payment Services

PO Box 47

Baltimore, Maryland 21235-0047

The Customer Service line is (410) 965-0607, use prompt number 6 to reach a representative. Customer Service Representatives are available Monday through Friday between 8:00 a.m. and 4:30 p.m. EST.

A telecommunications Device for the Deaf (TDD) telephone line is also available. The telephone number for the TDD line is 410-597-1395. The services available through the Financial Interactive Voice Response (FIVR) are available through TDD.

Treasury Electronic Payment Solution Contact Center at 1-800-333-1795

You can find your local office by going to the Social Security Office Locator on their website, at www.socialsecurity.gov/locator. Enter your postal zip code to get the address, telephone number, and directions to your local office.

Conclusion

Now is the time to start your retirement planning. It is never too soon. This information assisted me in successfully making my retirement plans and hopefully you will benefit from this guide.

Thanks for reading! If you enjoyed this book or found it useful I'd be very grateful if you'd post a short review on Amazon.com. Your support really does make a difference and I read all the reviews personally so I can get your feedback and make this book even better.

Thanks again for your support!

About the Author

Scotia Wade retired 2 years ago and now lives in North Carolina.

shairstonwade@gmail.com

www.facebook.com/boomersretirement

Check out other book by Scotia Wade

"100+ Budget Tips Guaranteed To Immediately Save You Money & Time"

http://www.amazon.com/dp/B01807QQNO

Made in the USA
San Bernardino, CA
20 June 2016